Bedtime Stories
for your
KITTY

Written By:
Herbert Kavet

Illustrated By:
Martin Riskin

Manufactured in the United States of America

30 29 28 27 26 25 24 23 22 21 20 19 18 17 16 15 14 13 12 11 10 9 8 7 6 5 4 3 2 1

Ivory Tower Publishing Co., Inc.
125 Walnut St., P.O. Box 9132, Watertown, MA 02272-9132
Telephone #: (617) 923-1111   Fax #: (617) 923-8839

Introduction

Cats sleep all the time. To be perfectly honest, no other pet needs bedtime stories less than a cat. It's safe to confess all this here in the Introduction. No one ever reads introductions, least of all in my books, where people only want to get to the cartoons. Perhaps years later, when you are rereading this book for the umpteenth time, you will notice this page and give it a perusal. By then, it will be too late. The book will be long paid for and all scuffed up, and it will be too late to return it.

hy This Book Was Written

"Another cat humor book?" you ask. Whole sections of bookstores are devoted to cat books. Entire chains of stores sell nothing but cat stuff. If the present output of cat books continues, there will be 4,200 cartoon books for every cat on the planet, and all the trees in Brazil and Oregon, not to mention Central Park in New York, will have been cut down to make them. But this one, of course, is different. It serves a real purpose. This book helps put your cat to sleep. Just suppose you have a pet that's having trouble getting his or her 23 hours of naps each day. There's nothing like taking your kitty onto your lap and reading a nice story or two to relax your pet and get him or her to doze off. With the help of this book, you might find your cat sleeping all the time, which will greatly cut down the time left for eating your plants, scratching your furniture and regurgitating hair balls.

Kitty Litter Lament

Kitty litter on the floor,
Kitty litter crunch some more.
It's really time to change the stuff,
Because the smell is getting rough.

Little
Cat Horner

Little Cat Horner
Sat in the corner
Eating a mouse she had caught.

She chewed on the tail,
Then spat in a pail,
And said, "I prefer food that's bought."

Hush-a-Bye Kitty

Hush-a-bye Kitty,
In the tree top,
The firemen won't come;
I should call a cop.

I'll put out some milk
And hope you'll come down,
'Cause tonight's so rainy
You'll probably drown.

The Three Little Piggy Cats

The three little piggy cats weren't called that because they were fussy eaters. Oh no, they would eat anything in sight and their table manners weren't so great either. They were called the three little piggy cats because all they did was think of food morning, noon and night. They were piggies all right, and their names were Puffball, Tiger and Sauce, and they lived with an old lady in a condo on Commonwealth Avenue in Boston.

One day Puffball awoke early and found the old lady had already filled their three bowls with liver by-products, vegetable gums and a bunch of chemicals whose names she could not pronounce. Puffball gobbled up her breakfast, nevertheless, and thinking it was yummy, proceeded to check out Tiger's bowl, just to make sure he didn't get more than her. Between checking and nibbling at Tiger's bowl, before long, it was empty. "Uh oh," thought Puffball, "Tiger will be apoplectic when he finds I've eaten his breakfast." Then she had an idea. "Why not eat Sauce's bowl, too, and pretend the old lady forgot to put out all our breakfasts?" And she did.

Tiger awoke hungry as ever and sauntered into the kitchen. You can imagine his surprise to see all their bowls empty. Finding nothing to eat and already feeling a little weak from hunger, he jumped out the back window to check the neighbor's garbage can. This morning was good hunting because under the Colombian coffee grounds, Tiger found the remains of a lobster dinner. Now, Bostonians know how to crack and eat lobster, but they still leave enough to keep a cat happy, and Tiger frolicked in the can for hours.

The Three Little Piggy Cats

Sauce awoke late and finding her bowl empty and the neighbor's garbage can picked clean, she started the day quite grumpy. Besides, the weather was humid and she was having a bad hair day. But Sauce was also the cleverest of the three and ran across the avenue to visit the back of the Legal Seafood Restaurant in the old Statler Building. She almost got killed crossing the street because Bostonians tend to drive like that.

Sauce had trouble getting into the restaurant. She huffed and she puffed, but as any idiot knows, you can't blow down brick walls, even those built under the eye of a greedy, politically appointed building inspector who would ignore any code violation for a color TV. Finally, Sauce crawled through an air vent and found herself in pig heaven. Fish heads and fish dinners were everywhere, and she ate and ate until she could eat no more. When she was ready to leave, Sauce found she could no longer squeeze through the vent. A kindly kitchen worker, who spoke no English, saw her struggling, picked her up and used her as a hood ornament on his 1968 DeSoto.

Peter, Peter, Seafood-Eater

Peter, Peter, seafood-eater,
Liked his bisque a little sweeter;
Put in clams and lobster shell,
It made his breath just smell like hell.

Hickory, Dickory, Dock

Hickory, dickory, dock,
The mouse ran up the clock.
The clock struck one,
The mouse fell down.
And Samantha caught her with one
mighty blow of her paw and smashed
the mouse into that great cheese-ladened
mouse hole in the sky.

*T*hen Samantha didn't know what to do with the dead mouse 'cause as bad as dry cat food (containing ground corn and gluten meal held together by fish by-products) was, she wasn't about to eat a squooshed dead mouse. She decided to give the mouse to her mistress as a little present, but got thrown out of the house for her efforts by the ungrateful, squeamish woman.

There Was A Crooked Cat

There was a crooked cat,
   And she ran a crooked mile,
Chased by a crooked dog
   That had a crooked smile.
She reached a crooked tree,
   And climbed it way up high;
The dog barked for so long
   That Cat thought he would die.

The Little Kitten That Could

The Little Kitten That Could lived in an old wooden house with about 18 other cats. I know that sounds like a lot of cats, but her mistress was the local Cat Lady. You know the lady, there's one in every neighborhood, to whom everyone brings the kittens and strays. The Cat Lady's husband thought they only had 14 cats, but she really had 18.

In the front hallway of the old wooden house stood a tall feathery fern. All the big cats could jump up and nibble on the fern which indeed had yummy-looking tender green leaves growing on all sides, but the little kitten could just gaze up at the fern in frustration. It seemed much too high for her to reach. One day, the little kitten was at that point in a cat's cycle where she felt she just had to devour some green plant matter. She walked slowly to the front hallway and gazed up at the feathering fern. "I think if I jump really high," said the little kitten, "I could reach that fern."

"I think I can, I think I can," said the little kitten over and over to herself. Then she started jumping, and each time she jumped a little higher and a little higher. "I think I can, I think I can," and closer and closer she got to the feathery leaves. Finally, she gave one extra mighty leap, almost grasping the leaf, but instead, crashed into the stem and knocked the whole plant over. "I thought I could, I thought I could," said the little kitten as she happily nibbled on the fern. When the Cat Lady came home and saw the mess the little kitten had made, she grew very angry and locked the Little Kitten That Could in the room with the kitty litter.

Cat Spone

Cat Spone could eat no bone;
  His dog thought fish obscene.
And so, betwixt them both,
  They licked the trash can clean.

Pat-A-Cat

Pat-a-cat, pat-a-cat,
  Give me a hug,
I hope my master
  Is getting my grub.

Rub me and stroke me
  Up safe on your lap,
After I've eaten,
  It's time for my nap.

Little Pussy

I like little pussy,
   Her coat is so warm,
And if I don't hurt her,
   She'll do me no harm.

But pull on her tail
   Or step on a paw,
And pussy will bite you
   And run out the door.

To Market

To market, to market,
    To buy some cat food,
Home again, open it,
    Before I'm unglued.

To market, to market,
    Let's buy some fresh fish,
Home again, home again,
    Look at them squish.

To market, to market,
    It's liver today,
Home again, home again,
    Who cares what I weigh?

The Three Alley Cats Gruff

Once upon a time, there were three alley cats who had to go over a little railroad bridge to get to some garbage cans behind a Chinese restaurant. Under the bridge lived an ugly troll. Now trolls, as everyone knows, are ugly beasts imported from Taiwan with flashy neon hair on top of their heads.

The Three Alley Cats Gruff

First to cross the bridge was the youngest alley cat. *Pit pat, pit pat* came her footsteps. "WHO'S THAT CROSSING MY BRIDGE?" roared the troll. "It's only I," said the little alley cat, "Little Alley Cat Gruff." "Well, I'm going to gobble you up," screamed the troll. But keeping her cool, the littlest alley cat said, "Oh, Mr. Troll, I'm much too skinny and boney for you to bother with. Why don't you wait for my fatter brother?" "Well, be off with you," said the troll, hating to pick too many bones out of his dinner.

A little later came the second alley cat. *Pit pat, pit pat* went his footsteps. "WHO'S THAT CROSSING MY BRIDGE?" roared the troll once again. "I'm going to gobble you up." "Oh please, Mr. Troll, you wouldn't want to gobble me up. I've been having gastric distress all week, if you get my drift," said Medium Alley Cat Gruff. "Why don't you wait for my fatter and healthier brother?" "Very well, be off with you," said the troll, who had a rather sensitive digestive system himself.

The Three Alley Cats Gruff

At last came MAX, Big Alley Cat Gruff, the biggest alley cat. *PIT PAT, PIT PAT* went the footsteps. Then the troll popped his head over the edge and threatened to gobble up the alley cat, but Max never heard him. Max thought the troll was a new cat toy and took him home and rolled him around in the sunny corner of the TV room for hours and chewed on his neck.

Old King Tease

Old King Tease
Was a Siamese,
And a merry old cat was he.

He drank from the john,
And when he would yawn
Had breath that would wilt a tree.

Old King Tease

Now Old King Tease
Wanted just to please,
But his breath would make your eyes tear.

He'd come for a kiss,
Thinking nothing amiss,
But his friends would all disappear.

The Little Cat With The Curl

There was a little cat
Who had a little curl,
Right in the middle of her tail.

The whole house understood
She was never very good,
Especially when chewing up the mail.

Ladycat

Ladycat, Ladycat, run away home.
Dinner is ready, it's no time to roam.
That stupid old dog, your food will dispose.
You'd best get there quickly and scratch
*   his big nose.*

ary Had A Kitty Cat

Mary had a kitty cat,
   Its coat was white as snow,
And everywhere that Mary went
   The cat was sure to go.

When Mary and her beau would smooch,
   Upon the parlor floor,
Her cat would sit and watch them both
   'Til thrown out the door.

Green Cats Eat Spam

Do you think green cats eat Spam?

I do not really give a damn.

Would they eat them with a clam,
Or perhaps a bit of jam?

I told you then, I'll tell you now,
I don't care what they do or how.

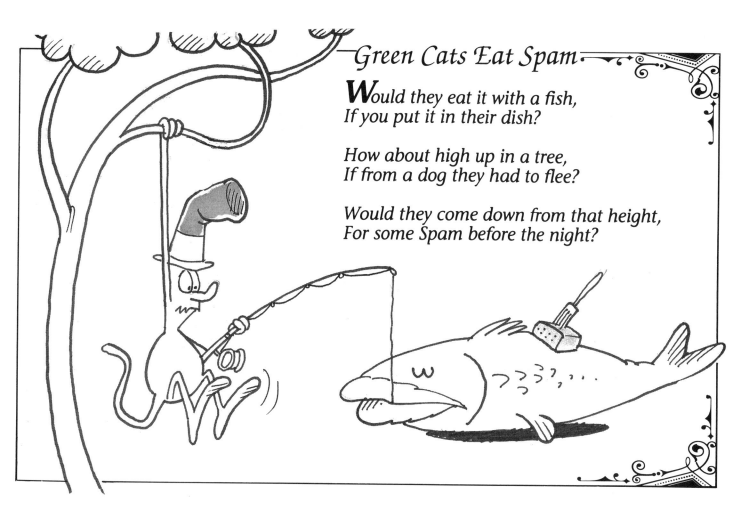

Green Cats Eat Spam

Would they eat it with a fish,
If you put it in their dish?

How about high up in a tree,
If from a dog they had to flee?

Would they come down from that height,
For some Spam before the night?

Green Cats Eat Spam

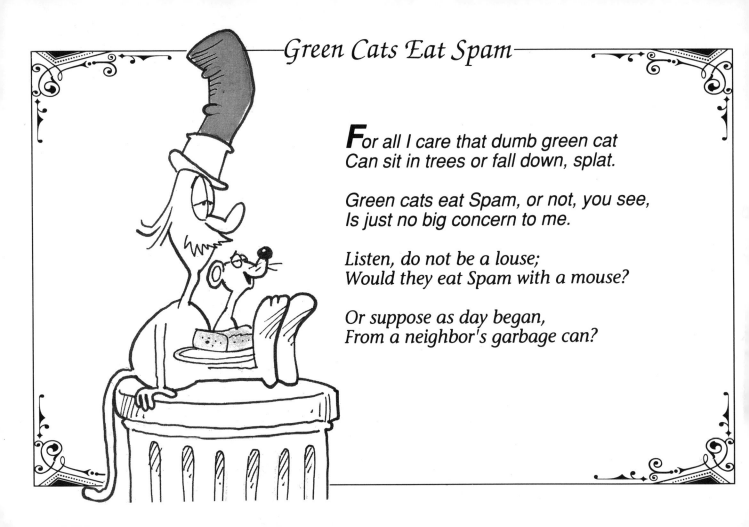

For all I care that dumb green cat
Can sit in trees or fall down, splat.

Green cats eat Spam, or not, you see,
Is just no big concern to me.

Listen, do not be a louse;
Would they eat Spam with a mouse?

Or suppose as day began,
From a neighbor's garbage can?

I've had enough, you make me sick,
Your head is just a bit too thick.

Just take your Spam and green cats, too,
And let me tell you what to do.

Bend over far and touch your toe,
And I will show you where to go.

Old Mother Hubbard

Old Mother Hubbard
Went to the cupboard
To give her cat, Calvin, a treat.

But when she got there,
The cupboard was bare,
So Calvin just sucked on his feet.

The Old Cat That Lived In A Shoe

There was an old cat
    Who lived in a shoe
With so many kittens
    She didn't know what to do.

With ads, signs and pleading,
    She broke all the rules,
And gave them away
    To some soft-hearted fools.

Taffy

Taffy was a Persian, Taffy was a thief;
Taffy in the kitchen, stole a piece of beef.

When I went to Taffy's place, Taffy was not home.
Taffy in the garbage can chewing on a bone.

Taffy

I thought she might be hungry,
   And always filled her dish,
Instead of eating cat food,
   She ate my pet goldfish.

Now I was getting angry with
   This naughty little pet,
So just to show her who was boss,
   I fixed her at the vet.

Missy Eats A Mouse

Missy had heard about mice, of course, but mostly in the form of cartoon characters on the TV she loved to watch. There were very few real mice on the 12th floor apartment where she lived. It wasn't until the family took her to a cabin on Lake George that Missy saw a real mouse.

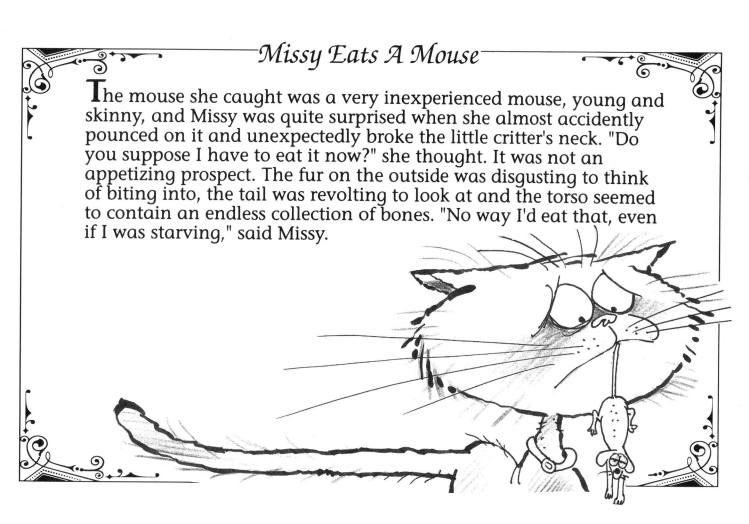

Missy Eats A Mouse

The mouse she caught was a very inexperienced mouse, young and skinny, and Missy was quite surprised when she almost accidently pounced on it and unexpectedly broke the little critter's neck. "Do you suppose I have to eat it now?" she thought. It was not an appetizing prospect. The fur on the outside was disgusting to think of biting into, the tail was revolting to look at and the torso seemed to contain an endless collection of bones. "No way I'd eat that, even if I was starving," said Missy.

So Missy decided to just leave the dead mouse where her mistress would find it. Missy even expected, perhaps, a small reward for her efforts. Then Missy ate the remainder of a peanut butter cracker and two green M & M's she'd found under the table, and took her 14th nap of the morning. Never again would she pounce on skinny mice.

Pussycat And The Queen

"*P*ussycat, Pussycat,
Where have you been?"

"I've been to London
To visit the Queen."

"And what did you do
In such fine company?"

"Why she talked of scandals,
And I scratched a flea."

Three Blind Mice

Three blind mice, three blind mice,
See how they run, see how they run.
They ran into walls and they ran into doors,
They were caught by a cat that had very sharp claws,
The cat ate them up and the taste left her sad,
Compared to dead mice dry cat food's not bad.
Three blind mice, three blind mice.

Jack Be Nimble

Jack, be nimble, Jack, be quick,
Jack jumps up a wall of brick.
See the birdies chirping near,
Jack can't reach them, that is clear.

Baa, Baa, Black Cat

Baa, Baa, Black Cat,
   Have you scratched a chair?
Yes, sir, yes, sir,
   It's the new one over there.

I've torn the cover
   And ruined the back,
Now when my mistress comes,
   She'll give me a whack.

Hey, Diddle, Diddle

Hey, diddle, diddle,
The cat and the fiddle,
My master's away for the day.

I'll play with the yarn,
And drink from the john,
And see if the curtains fray.

Curious Georgette Goes To The Vet

Curious Georgette was a darling, fluffy Angora who was always curious. Mostly, she was curious about male cats and this curiosity led to nine litters of kittens in the last four years. "Enough!" cried her mistress, "Enough!" cried her master. "Curious Georgette has had enough kittens. It's time to take her to the vet and get her FIXED."

Curious Georgette Goes To The Vet

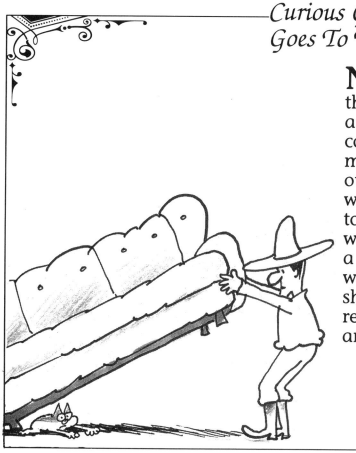

Now Curious Georgette was never thrilled to go to the vet in the first place and would hide under the living room couch whenever she heard the word mentioned. Her owners used to spell it out when they talked so Georgette wouldn't understand. "I think we have to take Georgette to the V-E-T," they would say. This worked at first, but after a few months, Georgette caught on. So when Georgette heard the letters 'V-E-T,' she high-tailed it into the furthest back reaches under the living room couch and fortified herself there.

Curious Georgette
Goes To The Vet

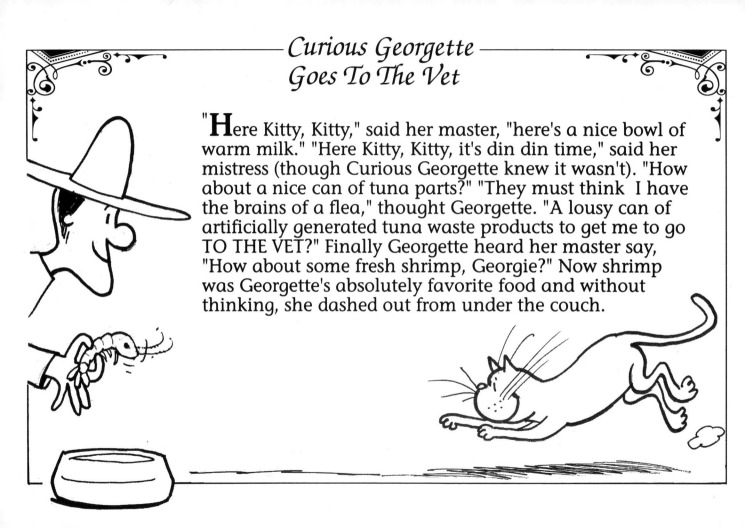

"**H**ere Kitty, Kitty," said her master, "here's a nice bowl of warm milk." "Here Kitty, Kitty, it's din din time," said her mistress (though Curious Georgette knew it wasn't). "How about a nice can of tuna parts?" "They must think I have the brains of a flea," thought Georgette. "A lousy can of artificially generated tuna waste products to get me to go TO THE VET?" Finally Georgette heard her master say, "How about some fresh shrimp, Georgie?" Now shrimp was Georgette's absolutely favorite food and without thinking, she dashed out from under the couch.

Curious Georgette Goes To The Vet

"Gotcha," Curious Georgette heard as she was firmly grasped. "Ha, ha, ha, we don't even have any shrimp," said the evil stepmother, as she stuffed Georgette into the oven—no, no, wait, that's the wrong fairy tale. What really happened is much worse. Curious Georgette was taken to the V-E-T and fixed, and spent the rest of her life nibbling ferns in the family room since she really didn't feel like going out with the guys anymore.

Sing A Song
Of Sixpence

Sing a song of sixpence
  The house is full of flies.
They're pretty hard to catch
  'Cause they have ten thousand eyes.

Butterflies are playthings
  That are a lot more fun.
I catch them when they fly too low
  And eat them in the sun.

Sing A Song Of Sixpence

My Master's in the TV room
With a football game.
Mistress is in the kitchen
Cooking with a flame.

The kids are in the garden
In a hole they dug.
Perhaps I'll walk around in it
And track it on the rug.

This Is the House Where Jack Slept

*T*his is the house where Jack slept.

This is the mouse
That crept into the house
Where Jack slept.

This is the smell
That cats know so well
Which came from a mouse
Who crept into the house
Where Jack slept.

This is the plant
Whose leaves are so scant
That stood near the smell
That cats know so well
Which came from a mouse
Who crept into the house
Where Jack slept.

This Is the House
Where Jack Slept

*T*his is the pot
That's shaped rather squat
That's all filled with dirt
And's ready to squirt
That's under the plant
Whose leaves are so scant
That stood near the smell
That cats know so well
Which came from a mouse
Who crept into the house
Where Jack slept.

This Is the House Where Jack Slept

This is the mess
Because, you can guess
When Jack sprang in haste
At the mouse he could taste
He hit the big pot
That's shaped rather squat
That's all filled with dirt
And's ready to squirt

That's under the plant
Whose leaves are so scant
That stood near the smell
That cats know so well
Which came from a mouse
Who crept into the house
Where Jack slept.

Three
Little Kittens

Three little kittens
All were smitten
By the new silk drapes in the hall.

"Oh, mother dear,
We sadly fear,
We've ripped them from the wall."

Three Little Kittens

"**Y**ou naughty kittens
Where is it written
That you should wreck this house?

"You'll go to bed
And not get fed
Unless you catch a mouse."

The Little Red Cat

One day the Little Red Cat was walking along and she found a tobacco seed. "Hmmmm," said the Little Red Cat, "this seed should be planted. Who will help me plant this seed?"
"Not I," said the Brown Dog.
"Not I," said the Little Goldfish.
"Not I," said the Pet Canary.
"Then I will," said the Little Red Cat and she did.

The Little Red Cat

In time, the seed grew into a tall healthy tobacco plant and the Little Red Cat thought it was time to pick it. "Who will help me pick the tobacco?" she asked.
"Not I," said the Brown Dog.
"Not I," said the Little Goldfish.
"Not I," said the Pet Canary.
So the Little Red Cat picked the tobacco leaves herself. When the tobacco was picked, it was time to dry it, and again when the Little Red Cat asked her friends, all she got was a "Not I" from the lazy dog, goldfish and canary, though it was doubtful that the goldfish would have been much help anyway, since he tended to lie there and flop when out of the water. But at least he could have been nicer about it.

Anyhow, to make a long story short, when it came time to make the tobacco into cigarettes, the stupid lazy dog, goldfish and canary all gave their damn "Not I" again, and the Little Red Cat was left with the job of rolling the cigarettes, which is hard enough for a cowboy with ten fingers, but a really tough job for a cat that's been declawed recently. But somehow she managed.

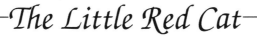

When the cigarettes were rolled and ready, the Little Red Cat said, "Who will go to the corner bar with me to smoke these cigarettes?" "Not I," said the Brown Dog, "it's time for my run." "Not I," said the Little Goldfish, "I have to lead the water aerobics class." "Not I," said the Pet Canary, "I have to get some seeds and whole grain at the health store." So the Little Red Cat smoked all the cigarettes herself, developed a little emphysema, high blood pressure and a cough you wouldn't believe, and was made to feel like a criminal whenever she lit up at a restaurant.

OXYGEN

The Cat Who Was Fat

There once was a cat
    That did nothing at all.
This cat loved to eat,
    And she looked like a ball.

This cat did not play.
    She just sat, sat, sat, sat,
And in between eating,
    Just grew very fat.

She always felt pleased
    When her bowl it was filled.
Dry food or wet food,
    They both left her thrilled.

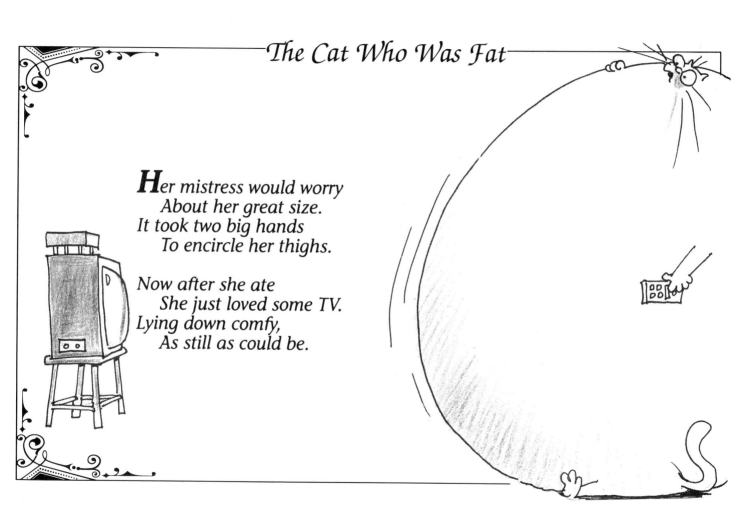

Her mistress would worry
   About her great size.
It took two big hands
   To encircle her thighs.

Now after she ate
   She just loved some TV.
Lying down comfy,
   As still as could be.

*T*hen one day her mistress
    Came into the house,
And carried a fur ball
    That wasn't a mouse.

Under her arm was
    A bright frisky pup,
And the cat that was fat
    Wondered just what was up.

"Now you two be friends
    And together you'll play."
The cat was so stunned,
    She had nothing to say.

The Cat Who Was Fat

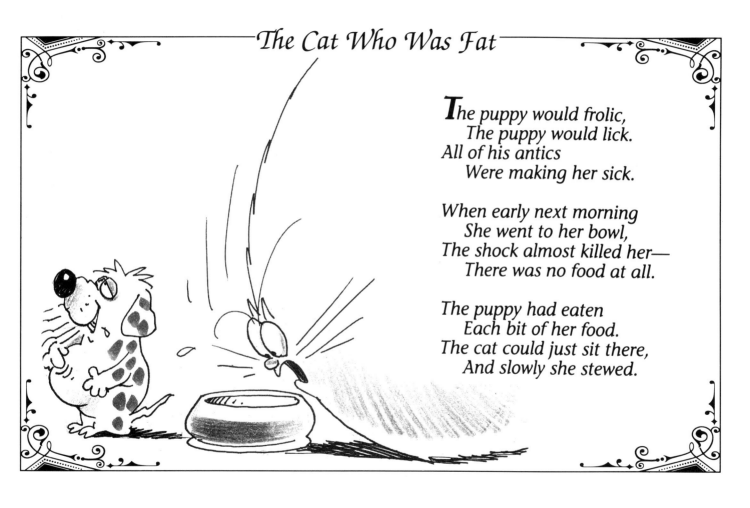

The puppy would frolic,
The puppy would lick.
All of his antics
Were making her sick.

When early next morning
She went to her bowl,
The shock almost killed her—
There was no food at all.

The puppy had eaten
Each bit of her food.
The cat could just sit there,
And slowly she stewed.

This ridiculous scene
    Was repeated at noon.
She grew weak with hunger
    And thought she would swoon.

Her weight it did plummet,
    This cat that was fat.
The puppy was starving her
    Just like a rat.

This puppy is trouble.
    This puppy must go.
But just how to do it,
    I really don't know.

Just when she thought she
   Could stand it no more,
Who should come sauntering
   Through the front door?

It was cousin Leo,
   A lion type cat,
And the pup took one look
   And decided to scat.

So if there's a puppy
   That's making you mad,
Get rid of him quick
   Or your life will be sad.

Goldisocks And The Three Teddy Bears

Goldisocks was an American Shorthair who lived with a family in a white house in Shaker Heights. The little girl in the family had a beautiful pink and blue room upstairs with three teddy bears on her bed. Now Goldisocks was a downstairs cat and she was not allowed up to the bedrooms. But one day when the family was away, her curiosity got the better of her and she crept upstairs.

You can imagine Goldi's surprise when she saw the three teddy bears. "What wonderful playmates they will make," she thought, and she jumped right up on the bed and started playing with the daddy teddy bear. Goldisocks played with the bow around the teddy bear's neck, and she played with the bear's big nose so much that eventually it fell off, but the daddy bear was too hard and too big for Goldi's taste.

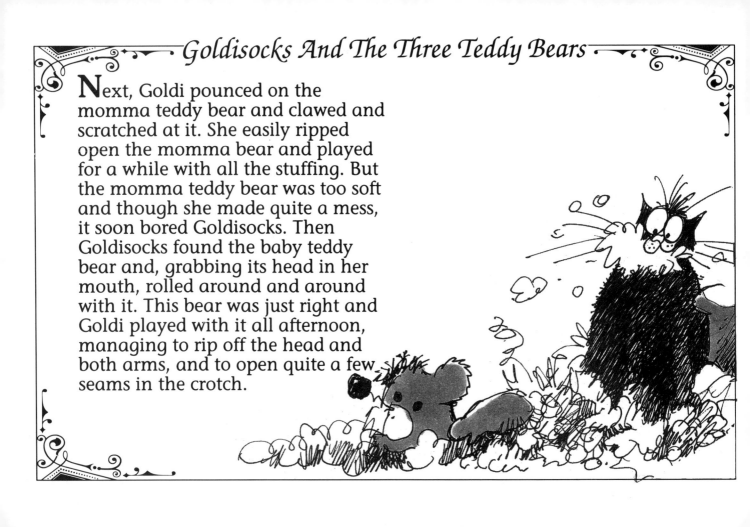

Next, Goldi pounced on the momma teddy bear and clawed and scratched at it. She easily ripped open the momma bear and played for a while with all the stuffing. But the momma teddy bear was too soft and though she made quite a mess, it soon bored Goldisocks. Then Goldisocks found the baby teddy bear and, grabbing its head in her mouth, rolled around and around with it. This bear was just right and Goldi played with it all afternoon, managing to rip off the head and both arms, and to open quite a few seams in the crotch.

When the little girl came home, she went to her room and found her daddy teddy bear minus his nose. Then she found her momma teddy bear or, I should say, the insides, spread all over the floor. The arms of her baby teddy bear were on the floor of her closet, but by this time she was so angry that she dumped her bowl of porridge over Goldisocks. Goldisocks had to spend the rest of the day licking herself clean, and early the next morning, she regurgitated a hair ball the size of Kansas.

Pussy Putter's Picture Book

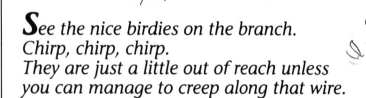

*S*ee the nice birdies on the branch.
Chirp, chirp, chirp.
They are just a little out of reach unless
you can manage to creep along that wire.

See the nice new silk pillow.
Mmmm, soft and fluffy.
What fun to jump on.
What fun to scratch all
that nice soft fabric.

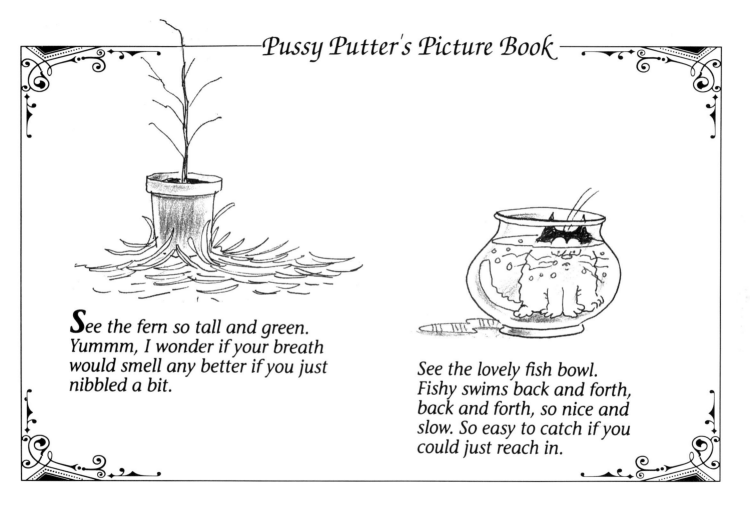

See the fern so tall and green. Yummm, I wonder if your breath would smell any better if you just nibbled a bit.

See the lovely fish bowl. Fishy swims back and forth, back and forth, so nice and slow. So easy to catch if you could just reach in.

Jack And The Beanstalk

Jack was an obedient cat who never had to be declawed and whose breath was sweet due to the dry cat food his mother fed him, which he really did not prefer to the expensive canned stuff. One day, his mother gave him a manufacturer's coupon for $.50 off a giant bag of kitty chow and sent him to the market. On the way, Jack ran into a hip cat named Duke, who hung around the corner and was the local dealer. Duke inquired as to Jack's errand and with the help of a chain saw, talked Jack into trading his money and coupon for three little white pills.

Jack And The Beanstalk

Jack took one of the little white pills as he walked along, and by the time he arrived home, he was seeing beanstalks growing everywhere, including out of his ears and tail, not to mention some very bright psychedelic colors. Jack was so high, it was easy for him to climb one of the beanstalks. "Who knows," he thought, "there might be a golden goose at the top or maybe even canned cat food made out of Beef Pulp and Poultry Digest, whatever that is."

Jack And The Beanstalk

Jack climbed way up to the top of the beanstalk. It ended in a cloud, and Jack jumped off and almost got knocked over by Henney Penney who was running around screaming, "The sky is falling! The sky is falling! We must run and tell the king." At the time, it seemed the right thing to do, so Jack joined Henney Penney, Goosey Loosey, Cokey Locky and the rest of the idiots, and went off to find the king.

Along the way, they came upon a fierce giant who growled when he saw them, and said, "Fe Fi Fo Fum, I smell the blood of an Englishman," which Jack noticed didn't rhyme very good at all. The chickens, ducks and geese all got frightened and flapped off, but Jack wasn't concerned about the giant smelling his blood, since the only smell he could notice was his kitty litter which hadn't been changed in three weeks. And besides, he was an American cat, so he wasn't scared at all. By this time, the effects of the little white pill were wearing off, and Jack thought it might be a good idea to get away from all these nuts and go back to the kitchen where perhaps lunch was waiting.

Jack And The Beanstalk

Jack walked back to the beanstalk, which looked pretty high up indeed and rather scary to climb down. Way below, he could see his mother calling the fire department, but he knew they never came anymore to rescue cats up trees, and as his head started to clear, he realized that it was a tree he was stuck in. He certainly hoped the police wouldn't come to help him, still a little spaced out and with those two other white pills in his pocket. So he stayed up in the tree until it got cold that evening and his mother put out a warm bowl of milk. When he came down, his mother cried and cried and grounded Jack for a month. The moral here, kitties, is to never talk to strangers and to never ever take little white pills from them.

ack And Jill

Jack and Jill were barn cats, and one day they went up the
hill. They didn't go up the hill for water or anything stupid like that.
Water you get from a faucet or at least a hose around a barn. They
went up the hill to get a little privacy 'cause Jill was in heat and
she wanted some action in the worst way.

When Jack and Jill got up the hill, they found a cozy spot and did "you know what" — after which Jill wanted to lay around and snuggle, but Jack said he was hungry and went looking for a pizza. Jack seldom felt romantic after sex.

A few weeks later when Jill was starting "to show," the farmer's wife got so angry, she ran after her with a carving knife and threatened to cut off her tail, but that's another story. With all the hubbub that Jill's pregnancy was causing (she had broken up with Jack by this point and had decided to move in with a friend and try her hand at being a single parent), the time just flew by and before long, the kittens were cuddling in the birthing box.

Jack, meanwhile, had taken up with an aerobics instructor from his club. When Jill ran into them one day at the mall and saw the floozie swishing her tight little body around, she lost her temper, whacked Jack with a can of Spaghetti O's and broke his crown.

Kitty Horror Stories

The stories that follow are likely to result in nightmares among kittens and their use should be limited to older cats. These stories are particularly appropriate for camping trips, and recounting them just before bedtime is a guarantee of having a snugly squirming cat in your sleeping bag the whole night through.

What Canned Cat Food Is Made Of

Long, long ago, a little cat named Star decided to read a canned cat food label. Although Gourmet Fish Feast was printed in bold beautiful type along with a picture of a very happy cat, Star found she had to look very carefully to find the actual ingredients. Now Star had very good eyes, but still she had to hold the can very close. What she saw frightened her. What do you suppose Fish By-Products are? You don't suppose they would feed me skin and intestines do you? And what's taurine? Do you suppose that has anything to do with the recent decrease in my sexual appetite?

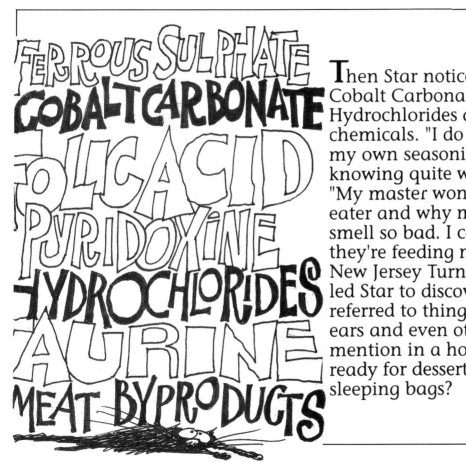

FERROUS SULPHATE
COBALT CARBONATE
FOLIC ACID
PYRIDOXINE
HYDROCHLORIDES
TAURINE
MEAT BYPRODUCTS

Then Star noticed the Ferrous Sulfate, Cobalt Carbonate, Folic Acid and Pyridine Hydrochlorides among 20 or 30 other chemicals. "I do wish they would let me add my own seasoning," thought Star, not knowing quite what all the names meant. "My master wonders why I'm such a fussy eater and why my farts and my breath smell so bad. I could tell him. The stuff they're feeding me sounds like parts of the New Jersey Turnpike." Further investigation led Star to discover that "By-Products" referred to things like snouts, lips, intestines, ears and even other things too horrible to mention in a horror story. O.K. kitties, who's ready for dessert before climbing into our sleeping bags?

The Alphabet Song

A, B, C, D, E, F, G,
How about a snack for me?
All of you are eating there,
I just get to sit and stare.
A, B, C, D, E, F, G,
Someone have some sympathy.

The End

Other books we publish are available at many fine stores. If you can't find them, send directly to us. $7.00 postpaid

2400-How To Have Sex On Your Birthday. Finding a partner, special birthday sex positions and much more.

2402-Confessions From The Bathroom. There are things in this book that happen to all of us that none of us ever talk about, like the Gas Station Dump, the Corn Niblet Dump and more.

2403-The Good Bonking Guide. Great new term for doing "you know what". Bonking in the dark, bonking all night long, improving your bonking, and everything else you ever wanted to know.

2407-40 Happens. When being out of prune juice ruins your whole day and you realize anyone with the energy to do it on a weeknight must be a sex maniac.

2408-30 Happens. When you take out a lifetime membership at your health club, and you still wonder when the baby fat will finally disappear.

2409-50 Happens. When you remember when "made in Japan" meant something that didn't work, and you can't remember what you went to the top of the stairs for.

2411-The Geriatric Sex Guide. It's not his mind that needs expanding; and you're in the mood now, but by the time you're naked, you won't be!

2412-Golf Shots. What excuses to use to play through first, ways to distract your opponent, and when and where a true golfer is willing to play.

2416-The Absolutely Worst Fart Book. The First Date Fart, The Lovers' Fart, The Doctor's Exam Room Fart and more.

2417-Women Over 30 Are Better Because... Their nightmares about exams are starting to fade and their handbags can sustain life for about a week with no outside support whatsoever.

2418-9 Months In The Sac. Pregnancy through the eyes of the baby, such as: why do pregnant women have to go to the bathroom as soon as they get to the store, and why does baby start doing aerobics when it's time to sleep?

2419-Cucumbers Are Better Than Men Because... Cucumbers are always ready when you are and cucumbers will never hear "yes, yes" when you're saying "NO, NO."

2421-Honeymoon Guide. The Advantages Of Undressing With The Light On (it's easier to undo a bra) to What Men Want Most (being able to sleep right afterwards and not talk about love).

2422-Eat Yourself Healthy. Calories only add up if the food is consumed at a table and green M&M's are full of the same vitamins found in broccoli.

2423-Is There Sex After 40? She liked you better when the bulge above your waist was in your trousers. He thinks wife-swapping means getting someone else to cook for you.

2424-Is There Sex After 50? Going to bed early means a chance to catch up on your reading and you miss making love quietly so as not to wake the kids.

2425-Women Over 40 Are Better Because... No matter how many sit-ups they do, they can't recapture their 17-year-old body—but they can find something attractive in any 21-year-old guy.

2426-Women Over 50 Are Better Because... They will be amused if you take them parking, and they know that being alone is better than being with someone they don't like.

2427-You Know You're Over The Hill When... All your stories have bored most acquaintances several times over. You're resigned to being overweight after trying every diet that has come along in the last 15 years.

2428-Beer Is Better Than Women Because (Part II)... A beer doesn't get upset if you call it by the wrong name; and after several beers, you can go to sleep without having to talk about love.

2429-Married To A Computer. You fondle it daily, you keep in touch when you're travelling and you stare at it a lot without understanding it.

2430-Is There Sex After 30? He thinks foreplay means parading around nude in front of the mirror, holding his stomach in; and she found that the quickest way to get rid of a date is to start talking about commitment.

2431-Happy Birthday You Old Fart! You spend less and less time between visits to a toilet, your back goes out more than you do and you leave programming the VCR to people under 25.

2432-Big Weenies. Why some people have big weenies while other people have teenie weenies; as well as the kinds of men who possess a member, a rod and a wang—and more!

2433-Games You Can Play With Your Pussy. Why everyone should have a pussy; how to give a pussy a bath (grease the sides of the tub so it can't claw its way out); and more!

2434-Sex And Marriage. What wives want out of marriage–romance, respect and a Bloomingdale's chargecard; what husbands want out of marriage –to be allowed to sleep after sex.

2435-Baby's First Year. How much will it cost, secrets of midnight feedings, do diapers really cause leprosy and other vital info for parents.

2436-How To Love A New Yorker. You love a New Yorker by pretending to understand their accent, sharing a parking space and realizing they look at "Out of Towners" as new income.

2437-The Retirement Book. Updates the retiree on Early Bird Specials, finding their bifocals and remembering things like paying for the book.

2438-Dog Farts. They do it under the table, in front of the TV, and after devouring some animal they caught in the yard. This book describes them all.

2439-Handling His Midlife Crisis. By treating him like a child when he wants to feel young again and consoling him when he goes from bikinis to boxer shorts.

2440-How To Love A Texan. You love a Texan by agreeing that their chili is just a mite hot, humoring them when they refer to their half acre as a ranch and rushing to help when their belt buckle sets off a security alarm.

2441-Bedtime Stories for your Kitty. Kitties love a story before bedtime and this book guarantees to keep their attention; Goldisocks and the 3 Teddy Bears, The 3 Little Kittens, and more.

2442-Bedtime Stories for your Doggie. This book of tales will keep big doggies as well as puppies entranced every night with stories like The 3 Billy Dogs Gruff, The Little Doggie That Could and many more.

2443-60 With Sizzle! When your kids start to look middle-aged and when your hearing is perfect if everyone would just stop mumbling.

Ivory Tower Publishing Co., Inc., 125 Walnut St., P.O. Box 9132, Watertown, MA 02272-9132   Tel: (617) 923-1111